NOT A CONTEST

HOW TO LOVE TEACHING

LOUISE PIERCE

LP PUBLICATIONS

Formatted by Ant Press - www.antpress.org

Published by LP Publications

This book is dedicated to my family, those living and those now on another plane.

My husband, Mark, my son, Stephen, my Mom and Dad.

My brother Robert – taken too soon - who told me to quit my stupid job and go back and get my teaching certification.

For Ginger, April and Bobby, All the Tomarellis, Coccos, the Shackletons and the Henshalls.

For the Pierces, Tolands, and my Uncle Tom, the first teacher I ever knew.

Without all of you, this wouldn't have been possible.

Thank you.

CONTENTS

Introduction vii

1. Love 1
2. Not Delivering Information 3
3. Nuts and Bolts of the Day 7
4. Personal Warmth 11
5. Thick Skin 15
6. Logic and Linear Progression 21
7. Administrators 25
8. Respect Support Staff 29
9. Have No Fear 33
10. Meet Them Where They Are 37
11. Modern References 43
12. Tune Out Noise 47
13. Unions 49
14. Being Organized 53
15. Don't Complain 57
16. Room Decor 61
17. P's and Q's 67
18. Power 73
19. Reading for Empathy 77
20. Not a Contest 81
21. The Only Constant is Change 85
22. Fortune favors the brave 89

Acknowledgments 91
About the Author 93

INTRODUCTION

As thousands (perhaps millions) of retired teachers before me decided to write a book, I joined the fray. Maybe they believed they had a great novel in them, and yes, several years ago, I started one of those too. Instead of that or a memoir about teaching, I decided to try to tell you all the things I wished someone had told me early in my teaching career. Things that would have saved me a great deal of anxiety and stress had I but known.

It's a bit of a memoir, of course, because it is all experience-based. But it is based on my experiences and not on educational research. I am aware, however, that what I impart to the reader may be found, in one form or another, in educational literature.

This book is for both new and experienced teachers who may need a bit of a lift. Teaching can be grinding. It can feel relentless. Sometimes things can happen in your personal life that make it really difficult to go in each day.

I lost my mother and brother within a year of each other. My whole nuclear family that I had known from childhood was gone, along with my mind. I was broken, and it was the middle of the school year.

Without supportive colleagues, I don't believe I could have done my job. My very good friend, Dan, was teaching the same classes, and each morning I would ask him what the lesson was for the day. He would tell me, and I would do it by muscle memory. By then, I'd been doing it for 25 years, but I couldn't generate it. He carried me through that year. Thank God for great colleagues and friends. I sincerely hope this book can be a good colleague and friend to you.

There are a couple of main points that the reader will see again and again but are described in different ways. Basically, they are the same. The first is that everything will be alright. Just stick to truly teaching; things will work out no matter what is going on with the principal, superintendent, or school board. And secondly, love the students and the subject matter.

Teaching is the best job in world. It truly is if one loves doing it. My former principal, Sean Hughes, said, "We are educating our one truly natural resource - our children." Thanks Sean.

For many years, politicians and specific segments of society have tried very hard to blame teachers for society's ills. They accuse us of being overpaid and being "liberals". As long as it deflects society's ills from them, and the decisions they have made and put into practice.

As teachers, we have very little control over what we teach. In some cases how we teach it and the socio-economic group we are teaching. That's not to say we have no power. We do but in a much smaller way than we are often given credit for.

What I will say, though, is that this pandemic has made it very apparent that we are essential and necessary for several reasons. Babysitting and providing a safe place for children and teens to go to during the day is probably number one. But the online chatter has revealed that there is no substitute for a real teacher to teach children subject matter.

In addition, I'm hearing from my many friends still in teaching that students returning to school after the pandemic are missing a lot of the social skills that are necessary to function productively in the world. It appears that proper behavior and being members of a civilized society are something that teachers also instill in their students. So, the world should never undervalue what teachers do. We are way more important than most people want to have us think we are.

While knowing one's own worth is essential, it is also important to be good at one's job. Every day we should do the best we can. When I first started teaching at the age of thirty, I soon realized I could no longer go out with my friends on a weeknight, if that included drinking or staying out late. When I was in advertising, I could dial in a day if I had been out the night before. I might be spaced out, or a little hung over.

Not so with teaching. One needs to be present in every moment. It is vital. Students' safety and well-being are in teachers' hands. Own the moment but try to do so with joy. You can still have fun on weeknights, of course you can. Just remember what is waiting for you the next day.

In Richard Russo's book, "Straight Man" (this refers to the comedic sense, not so much gender identity or sexual orientation), he's writing about the character's father, who is a fairly famous writer and has been given a chair at

Columbia University. When he goes to deliver his first lecture there, he freezes up and has to let his Teaching Assistant deliver the lecture. He writes,[1] "Out there by the door he could hear the manner in which the lecture was read, the vacillating timbre and skewed emphasis of the words as they came out of his assistant's throat, and he understood more poignantly than ever before the difference between delivering information and teaching." I have a chapter named "Not delivering info". I had written that even before reading this book because it is a very important distinction.

Over the years, I have heard many competent teachers talk about delivering information and it always made my eyes cross a little. Yes, teachers are delivering much-needed information to the students, but they are doing so much more. They are connecting, coaching, instructing, and imparting their passion for the subject as well. Anyone and just about anything can "deliver information". Many jobs across this country have been replaced by robots. Yet, as we can see from the teacher shortage, nobody is suggesting we use robots to teach! They need us. They can't replace our humanity, they never could, and frankly, they never will.

As a teacher, one is so much more than books, tablets, and TV. And THAT is what one should remember and work on doing. This is what I hope this book will help teachers do.

---

1. Richard Russo, "Straight Man", Random House Publishing Group, 1997-06-08

1
LOVE

The first thing to talk about as a teacher is love. Yes, you read that right, love.

You need to love your fellow human beings enough to care to teach them something. You need to love the subject(s) that you teach enough to care to impart that knowledge to your fellow human beings.

Love will get you through all the bad things about teaching. Love will enhance all the good things. This is a profession based on human contact, and if you don't embrace it all with genuine love, it is not the profession for you.

Sure, you can learn things from a book or computer. So much so that there is constant talk of teachers being replaced by computers. Unenlightened people believe that such replacement is possible and maybe even a good thing.

But education is about so much more than relaying information. First and foremost, it is about human connection. If the pandemic taught us anything at all, it taught us that.

What exactly am I talking about?

Think back to your own education. Why did you choose to be whatever you are? What were your favorite subjects? What classes did you do well in?

Now think about the teachers who taught those classes or influenced you along the way. What made those connections happen? In most cases, I believe you'll find it was because you connected with the teachers who taught those subjects most effectively. In some cases, it may be in spite of them. Anger and frustration can sometimes be motivating. But usually, it's because those subjects were taught by people who had a passion for their subject. They were able to communicate that to you and to connect to you in a human, basic way.

So, teaching with love in your heart that's the first basic thing you need to know. I once had a colleague, Ben, say to me, "You've always taught from the heart." I was kind of shocked. It took me a minute to grasp what he said. But once I did, I found it to be a great compliment. It meant I cared and connected. It's what one needs to do when teaching.

2
NOT DELIVERING INFORMATION

In my introduction, I quoted Richard Russo realizing that he understood the difference between delivering information and teaching. The difference is incredibly important. There are lots of ways to deliver information that doesn't require a teacher. But being taught is much more different than simply being given information. Let me illustrate my point.

Several years ago, we had a teacher come to us from another profession. Linda (not her real name) had worked in industry as a professional mathematician. Her knowledge of the world, which was extensive, was geared towards a business setting. She then became a teacher.

For a couple of years, the students constantly complained about her. Parents were calling the school, and it was very much a shit show. She had been evaluated as a teacher and had passed. Her work, as far as her preparation and her knowledge of the subject, was very good. Linda was "delivering the required information". So what was the problem?

My principal asked me to observe her class to see if I could figure it out and maybe help. So I did. What I saw was a person who knew her subject matter extremely well but didn't know how to connect with people.

When students entered the classroom, there was no welcoming smile, no "how are you". Instead of starting the class with, "How has your day been?" Or "Hello, I hope you're having a good day so far," she just went straight into the subject. There were no anecdotes about anything, no asides, no jokes, no small-talk. There weren't even any smiles.

When she asked if students had questions, it wasn't done in a way that genuinely invited the asking of questions. No, "Is this clear? Do you know what I'm saying?" No eye contact or waiting for nods. Just, "Does anyone have any questions?" It was very mechanical, subject-focused, and no-nonsense.

She also limited bathroom visits to three per semester, and students had a pass that recorded how many times they had used it. (PLEASE never do this.) So I observed the entire lesson, filled with good, concise, clearly explained information, while most of the students looked like they wished they were anywhere else.

I reported to the principal that Linda was not doing anything wrong. But she was not doing much right as far as teaching goes. Linda had no personal warmth. She didn't give them any of her personality or make connections with the students in a personal way.

I have to say that I also sensed fear in her, which I didn't tell the principal. I think a lot of her behavior was because she was afraid of losing control of the class. So Linda kept things very strict and dry, so nothing could vary behavior-wise.

Our principal, bless the man, took Linda under his wing and worked with her. He got her to take a couple of classes and personally tutored her on how to be with students. And she listened, for which I give her immense credit. I'm happy to report that Linda is still at her job and doing very well and is a respected member of the faculty.

What this story illustrates is how important one's teaching technique is. How do you make students comfortable enough to learn? It's pretty simple, really. Be a human being.

Smile. It doesn't matter what is happening in your life; put it aside; you are at work. These students don't know or care about what is happening in your home. Your job is to teach them. But, if something truly awful happens, a death in the family, etc., and you are struggling because of it, tell your students. Usually, they will be sympathetic and, for a while at least, excuse your feeling bad.

Talk to them like they are someone you are selling something to because you are. You are selling them your knowledge and the information they need to know. Make sure, when you ask for questions, you make eye contact. Wait, and phrase it in a friendly way. Project your voice from your sternum and pitch it in a warm manner so they can hear you AND feel the love.

Be confident, even if you are faking it. No one wants you to be a good teacher more than the students do. No one wants you to fail, especially them. Students WANT to be engaged; they want to learn. Oh, you have a few bad apples now and then, but if you are confident enough, you will bowl even those students over.

The longer I taught, the fewer discipline issues I had. Because I didn't take it personally (that's a big one) and because I

KNEW, I knew what I was doing. The power struggle is on your side, it is YOUR classroom, and the vibe in it is one YOU create.

Over the years, I taught many, many really intelligent students. Many were smarter than I was, and they knew it. But what I had and what they lacked was my education and my passion for my subject. And, of course, my experience. It doesn't mean you know everything. Please be sure to know you don't know everything and freely admit it. But be open to finding what information you lack and coming back with it the next day.

Once in a while, a kid can teach you something you don't know. Be open to that too. You will be challenged, especially by intelligent students, but this is not a battle you are engaged in; it is a love fest. So if a student challenges you, hear them out. But also let them know the parameters they and you are working in.

Sometimes their ideas aren't applicable. Sometimes their ideas are just crazy. But try not to shut them down in front of the class. Just say, "I hear you, and let's talk about this later when the class is working or after the lesson." Then you can explain why whatever they want is not going to work.

Sometimes, their ideas are good, and you can use them. Be sure to give them credit because no one wants to be taught by a credit hog.

3
NUTS AND BOLTS OF THE DAY

When you are a teacher, it is essential to be ON TIME. This was a struggle for me. Our day started at 7:30 am. When I say started, I mean I had to hit the ground running. There was no homeroom to wake up in. It was go time.

I am a night person and rarely go to sleep before 11 pm. People would tell me they were in bed at 9 pm. I was like, whaaat? I haven't been to sleep at 9 pm since I was ten years old. If that is how you are, more power to you. But if you are like me, you need to take care of yourself in other ways.

I would make my lunch the night before and have it packed and ready to grab from the fridge. Or I would shop at the weekend and buy pre-made food and have it bagged and in the fridge, ready for Monday morning. Then I would stock the fridge at work with food for the week.

Cook enough healthy food on a Sunday and make snack bags of things you like, such as carrots, pretzels, or whatever gets you through the day.

Lay out your clothes the night before. Check the weather report and have all the essentials lined up. I would set my alarm for 6 am then hit the snooze button until about 6:15 am. I would get up and shower. (If you can shower the night before, good for you.) If I don't shower in the morning, there is no point in me being upright because I am still asleep.

I put on my laid-out clothes, brush my teeth and hair, put on my jewelry (picked out the night before), and apply a swipe of mascara. I grab my lunch while making a cup of tea in a go-cup, and then I'm out the door. Ninety-nine percent of the time, I am at school no later than 7:25 am. I also lived ten minutes from school, a calculated decision. We moved there to shorten my commute. That is something to consider when choosing where to live. Remember you are going to have to commute! I arrive, sign in, and go up to the classroom. I get myself settled and ready to begin the day.

Be sure to greet the students when they come in. High schoolers are rarely cheerful at 7:30 am, so don't add to their moroseness. We'd get started. I'm swigging tea the whole time, and luckily, in our building, the students are allowed to imbibe what they want too.

I never objected to food or drink in my classroom unless the students left a mess. I always gave a very clear lecture at the beginning of the year about cleaning away their food and drinks at the end of the lesson. If they didn't, the privilege would be revoked. In my thirty years of teaching, I only had to do that twice.

As the students worked, I would eat breakfast, usually at my desk, and something small. I didn't really need much because we had lunch at 10:30 am. I usually ate my lunch in our Department Office, which was next to my classroom. It gave me a chance to talk to grown-ups, but I could also hear what was going on as students could be in our classrooms at lunch, and we had to keep an eye out. Then on with the rest of the day.

Highly recommended is staying on an extra half hour at the end of the teaching day. I know some schools insist their teachers do that. I found it really helpful and actually relaxing. It's a great time to get things tidied and ready for the next day. It gives you the time to get done anything you didn't get finished that day, such as answering emails and also having a chat with co-workers if you are so inclined. I know many people like to get to work an hour or half an hour early in the morning for the same reasons.

It's hard if you have kids of your own. When my son was little, as soon as I could, I had to run out after school. Instead, I would try to get to work a little bit early, but, as mentioned above, that isn't me. Do whatever works best for you.

Teaching, as we all know, is never confined to the hours you are in the classroom with students. I did most of my grading and lesson planning at home. I am more comfortable and relaxed there, and why not?

4
PERSONAL WARMTH

Over my years of teaching, I learned that personal warmth is something people are either blessed with or not. Some people just make you comfortable when you meet them. Some, not so much. We just know it when we meet someone who has personal warmth.

But here's the thing. If you're not blessed with personal warmth, you can work on it. It's little things, like beginning a lesson with, "How is everyone today?" Or, "You won't believe what happened to me on the way to school today!" Or, "I saw a great movie over the weekend, blah, blah, blah, has anyone one seen it?" It's letting the students in your class know you are a HUMAN BEING.

I've actually had students thank me for being a human being. Can you imagine? You need to be professional, but you also need to share your feelings. If something wonderful or terrible happens in your life, share it with the students. Some teachers don't acknowledge feelings when teaching, either theirs or the students, and it makes them seem like robots. The thing we have going for us is that teachers are not robots. It also lets students know you look at them as human beings and care about them.

Whenever possible, try to see the students as individuals. If someone abuses a privilege, then do something about that student. You don't start out punishing everyone for something that hasn't happened yet. Don't make blanket assumptions or rules in response to things that may never happen.

Another critical thing to remember is to acknowledge what is happening in the world. I know we are often uncomfortable talking about things like politics etc., and we shouldn't show any bias. I know some teachers do, and I think it's unprofessional. But we also don't live in a little bubble. If something big is happening in the world, acknowledge it. You don't have to get into a big discussion about it.

For instance, when the Black Lives Matter protests were going on, we were teaching remotely. In my weekly assignment email to students, I wrote something about the protests, just a basic acknowledgment of what was going on. I had several students write to thank me for that.

Just saying, yes, this is the world we are living in right now. I know it's hard to focus on what we're doing in class because of it, but let's give it a shot. Let's keep going because what else is there to do?

You can also ask the students if they want to talk about something that's going on. If the three previous classes have already discussed whatever it is, the students may just want to work and forget about it. But it's important to ask.

I taught through Columbine, many school shootings, 9/11, wars, and many upheavals. I learned that it's important to let students know your room is a safe space and let them talk if they want to. You don't know what kind of trauma or post-traumatic stress disorder students carry.

When Columbine happened, I had several survivors of a horrific plane crash that occurred over an elementary school. These children were in the schoolyard when a plane and helicopter collided above them during their recess. Our United States Senator, John Heinz, was killed in that crash. Burning fuel and plane parts flew out of the sky, injuring and killing several children below. It was remarkable more weren't injured, and that was due to alert playground staff.

When Columbine happened, these children, who had been in first and second grade at the time, were now in high school. Several of them spoke of how seeing the images of Columbine on television, the lines of kids running out of the building, etc., made them flashback to the crash. It was surprising and made me realize how deeply and for how long we carry trauma within us.

All this seeming digression gets us back to the personal warmth issue. Personal warmth is what helps make students trust us. And that trust is important. If you hold any personal prejudices against color, creed, sexual orientation, political party, etc., you need to fix yourself quickly or get out of teaching.

Are you going to like some students more than you like others? Of course you are. But just like a parent who might like one child better than another, you have to love them all the same. You first have to make them feel comfortable and calm and let them trust you.

Does this take time from you "delivering information"? Yes, yes, it does. Do you always make a connection with every student? Nope. Sometimes, despite your best efforts, you just don't connect. And that's okay; hopefully, they will connect with someone else in the building. But you must not stop trying.

When schools were closed during the global pandemic, the number one complaint from students was that they missed being in the classroom. They missed being with their friends and teachers and the personal connections. While we did our best to teach over zoom or video, it was not the same. It is difficult to really convey personal warmth or make connections when we are not face to face in real life.

If this has taught us anything about teaching, it is that nothing can replace a soft tap on the shoulder, a quick smile, or a comforting word of encouragement. These are things that tell us someone cares about us. It is something a teacher needs to learn how to do if it doesn't come naturally.

5
THICK SKIN

As a teacher, you need to develop a seriously thick skin. I know this isn't easy for most of us. Teachers are often kind, sensitive people, conscientious and caring about what others think. Unfortunately, if you want to survive in the profession, you need to stop caring about what others think of you.

I remember walking down the halls during my first year of teaching high school and being so incredibly self-conscious that I couldn't look at anybody. Then I realized that there was so much self-consciousness in the air that I was absorbing it.

Teenagers are ridiculously self-conscious. I'm a little bit of an empath, which of course, aggravates matters. I had to consciously steel myself to look at everyone and greet people. This was a great revelation because I couldn't figure out why I was so ridiculously uncomfortable.

The most important thing to recognize is that not everyone will like you. Whether you teach kindergarten or twelfth grade, students and staff are just people. Just as you don't like everyone you meet (often for reasons that aren't really rational), some of these people are not going to like you. AND THAT IS OKAY. Everyone doesn't have to like you.

You have to like you. If you are comfortable in your own skin, it will make other people more comfortable around you. If you don't like a student, the feeling is often mutual, and that may be part of why you don't like them. It may be that students are so shy, so awkward socially, that they don't emote at all around you. I sometimes personally mistook that for dislike. As is so often the case, I wish I knew then what I know now.

Don't assume someone doesn't like you just because they act strangely around you. Some people are just that way. The point is, even when I knew students didn't like me, I still treated them with love and compassion, as I would all the students. Sometimes that even won a student over. The same applies to adults.

If you find yourself concerned about people liking you, it will impede your ability to do your job. I don't have a step-by-step method to make you care less about what people think of you. For me, it was something I had to practice for a long time. It's only natural to want to be liked.

The perverse thing is most people who don't care if they are liked ARE liked. It's because they exude confidence. And confidence is essential in teaching. You have to have confidence in yourself to be a good teacher. Not misplaced confidence like never admitting you don't know something or that you are wrong. I mean just believing in yourself and loving yourself enough to stand in front of a room full of people and say what you have to say. If you don't have confidence, fake it till you make it.

A woman named Amy Cuddy did a Technology Entertainment Design (TED) talk called Fake it Till You Make it. It's mostly about body language, how you present yourself etc., that can signal to the world whether you are confident. It's worth the fifteen minutes to watch on YouTube.

Think about the people you've admired as teachers. Did they seem tentative and afraid? Probably not. Once you get going on the subject you are passionate about, you probably will forget you're talking to a room of resentful fourteen-year-olds and just make the magic happen.

Over the years, you will hear criticisms: that you did this, you did that, you don't like me, you need to do this better, etc., etc. What I can tell you is, accept constructive criticism, check that it is valid and try not to be defensive. Make changes or apply what has been said to your teaching.

Try to ignore the whining, complaining, or downright ridiculous criticisms. Complaints from students may be whatever is actually wrong with them. It might be something their parents said. It could be manipulation or, quite often, a misunderstanding. It will usually clear itself up if you have a discussion and can tease out the truth.

The same is usually true of adults. A calm, thoughtful discussion can often clear up any unintended misunderstandings that may lead to criticism about you.

As for the public at large, DO NOT GET ON THE SOCIAL-MEDIA PAGE OF THE COMMUNITY WHERE YOU TEACH. People will be saying ridiculous things without basis, and it will upset you. Just ignore it. The politics and opinions of your district are not your concern. Just do your job. If someone really comes after you, from the outside or the inside, let your union handle it.

Always try to teach somewhere with a union. It is what they are for, to defend you when things go very wrong. They will give you representation if you are guilty of something but will not shield you from the consequences. That is a fallacy. If you are not guilty, they will represent you and keep you safe from harm. If you have no union, find a senior teacher who can help you navigate through the troubled waters.

As to the country as a whole, they will say insane things about teachers. Do not pay attention and do not engage. It is not your problem. It is theirs. Move along.

Here is another thing while on this topic. Do not listen to rumors. Schools are rumor mills. As a union rep. I used to have people ask me about this and that rumor. Ninety-nine percent of the time, the stories had no basis in fact or such a small kernel of truth as to be unrecognizable.

Do not gossip or spread rumors. It's hard, I know, to stay away from gossip. It makes you feel part of the group. It can be fun to listen to, but it is inevitably harmful. To you most of all. You can be friends with your colleagues without being a gossip and rumor-monger. These things are damaging to you, your colleagues, and your profession.

Don't engage. If cornered, listen, smile, or show shock, whatever the appropriate emotion, then get away as soon as possible but don't say anything. Rumors and gossip always bite YOU in the ass. You are a professional. Always behave like one.

In short, do your job to the best of your ability, incorporate constructive criticism when you can and ignore the rest.

Having fun and teaching your students is the most important thing you must do daily. The rest is just distraction.

6
LOGIC AND LINEAR PROGRESSION

When I started teaching Art at the school where I taught, I did not have a set curriculum. My colleagues had designed their own, and that was helpful, but each year I had to figure out what I was teaching and why. No one ever questioned this.

Later in my career, we would get all the levels and schools together and, in a logical way, hash out an understanding of what we were trying to make sure the students knew. We wrote a very broad outline, so teachers could interpret it in their own way and with their own projects.

We were fortunate in this, but it also made for more work. I would sometimes wish someone would just hand me a textbook and tell me what next to teach. But I know that in reality, I wouldn't have liked that.

I know most teachers don't enjoy that kind of freedom. State mandates and textbooks, amongst others, tell teachers what to do, what to teach, and where they should be at what time of the year. If you have any freedom at all, ensure your curriculum is logical and builds on what was taught before, either by you or someone else. I think it's most confusing for students if there is no logical, linear progression. I believe it makes them uneasy and turns them off.

I'm not talking about plodding along monotonously or doing nothing spontaneously. Spontaneity is wonderful in the classroom, and you should make the most of it. When something important is happening in the world, bring it in, do a project about it, watch it on TV, and acknowledge its importance.

Sometimes in the dead of winter, I would take a class outside to build a snowman or make a snow sculpture. Sometimes we would collect rocks and leaves to draw. It was just something to do to break up the grinding inside-life so typical of January and February.

It may seem like nothing important got done that day, but it can make a big difference. Getting students outside is enormous, especially for high schoolers and middle schoolers who don't have recess or a way to blow off steam. I know not everyone can do this, but if you can, please do.

For those who can't go outside, don't be afraid to get them up and moving around in your room or in the school. Take students on a little walk through the school or make them jump up and down at their desks. It causes a bit of mayhem, but it gets their blood flowing and their brains working. Some will complain, but most enjoy it, and the complainers usually end up joining in and enjoying it too.

In the middle of my career, I took an Art History class while working on my Masters in Education. It was a really cool class taught by an archeologist. I was very excited and told my principal, Jack, about it at the time. He wondered if the school should run an Art History class. I said they had had one before my time, but it had died out.

He wanted it to be exciting, not a class where students looked at slides and memorized dates. His stipulation was no textbooks. I was all for it. Of course, I had to invent it as well. It was a ton of work, but I really enjoyed it. It was divided into two separate offerings, Cave Art to the Renaissance, then the Renaissance to Present Day. Each was a semester-long.

I found resources, videos (before computers), and books from which to copy pages, prints, and slides. The course evolved over the years, and, of course, once we had computers and projectors, it was so much easier.

I also introduced a hands-on component. We did an art project for every major period of time or movement. So for the Middle Ages, for instance, I taught students to embroider. This turned out to be remarkably popular. One wouldn't think it, but boys liked it as much as the girls. For some, it became a passion that they continued to pursue.

Many of the students in Art History were not Art students either, so it was a really nice mix of kids. I probably worked harder on that class than any other I taught, but, in many ways, I also found it the most rewarding.

Later, a new supervisor wanted to offer the class as an Advanced Placement (AP) subject, and they wanted me to teach it. I went to friends who taught AP History in the school and asked them what they thought I should do. AP Art History would require a textbook, lots of memorization, and of course, the big AP test at the end. I knew it would bring in a lot more students from around the school, but I was wary.

When I asked the folks who taught AP History if they thought I should do it, they answered with a resounding NO! They told me it would kill everything I loved about the class. The discussions that broke out, the written dissections and observations the students did, the little hands-on projects, and the detours we would take if we found things interesting that weren't initially in the lesson.

Knowing it would turn the subject into exactly what my former principal Jack and I didn't want it to be, made my mind up for me. I was never sorry about that decision because I don't believe the AP class would have brought the students any more joy than it would have for me.

If it seems I have gone entirely off target here, I haven't. The point is to keep students engaged, comfortable, and learning. Whatever that takes, and is legal, is what a teacher must do. If you need to change curriculum mid-stream to make sure something is clear and well-learned, then without putting yourself in jeopardy, you should do it. If it requires approval, do everything you can with a sound, data-driven argument to make that happen. The students' learning and happiness are the most important things.

7
ADMINISTRATORS

Administrators can be (a) Really Great, (b) Bland and Chicken-Hearted (c) Total Jerks. Just like everyone else in the world. I was lucky with my first and last principal. The first one I had for five years, the last for about twelve. Most of my career was spent with an outstanding principal. In between, I had a decent one, then a total jerk. The jerk didn't last, and they usually don't.

Assistant principals can play a significant role, or small one, depending on how your school is run. We usually had four, one for each grade level, depending on how populated the school was at the time. They, too, can run the gamut of personalities and expertise. Most, in my experience, have been really helpful.

I had one who was a complete saboteur and hated me for some reason. On the last day of school, before the summer break, she came to do my evaluation with students. REALLY?! She put crappy stuff in the evaluation about things she knew nothing about. I returned it, saying that I was signing it under protest. I didn't get an unsatisfactory or anything. But in thirty years, it was the only evaluation I received that was anything but glowing.

This same assistant principal did several other things that were just so blatantly wrong to me. I never said anything to the higher-ups. But, after a couple of years, she asked to go back into the classroom, and no one was more relieved than I.

Here's the most important thing to know about administrators. They come and go. Do your job, and they will leave you alone. If you don't show up on their radar, they won't come looking for you. Administrators are usually overwhelmed with either ridiculous or important things. What you do in your classroom doesn't even cross their minds. This is as long as you are not bringing things to their attention, such as complaints or anyone getting hurt. If you are doing something extraordinarily good, send them an email, maybe a photo. If they want to come to see it, they can. If you win an award, send them an email. Otherwise, try to keep your head down and do your job.

If you need their help, send them an email. If it can't wait, call their secretary and make an appointment. They don't want to be bothered, really, they don't. They are the middle management of education and are getting screamed at by everyone. The thing I tried most to do was to lighten their load. They might not acknowledge it, but they appreciate it.

Also, don't expect compliments or attaboys. Some schools do that, but many don't. Mine didn't. You were EXPECTED to be excellent. Once you get used to that, there is a certain pride in just maintaining excellence, to the best of your ability, without any congratulations. If you crave a lot of praise, education is definitely not for you.

Politicians have made us the scapegoats for society's ills, and the public pays our salaries but resents every penny. Get used to it. A few rare individuals will give you kudos for what you do. Most importantly, you need to do this job because you really want to, not because someone always tells you how great you are.

If you have wonderful administrators, revel in it. Enjoy their company when you see them. Help them out whenever you can or if they ask. If you have a so-so administrator, just avoid them and do your job. Have some kind of relationship, but stay away. That type can not be trusted. If you have a jerk, at all costs, don't let them see you think they are jerks. Be cordial but stay away as much as possible. Apologize as needed and keep your head down.

In my experience, bad administrators were usually moved on quickly or move on themselves. They are not happy in themselves is the key. Sometimes it's that they have been brought in to "clean up" a situation and think they're the new sheriffs in town. Let them strut and posture but once again, just do your job. It is not your business.

This goes for the school board, superintendent, curriculum supervisors, etc., etc. Most of them are scrabbling their way up the ladder or down it. Don't let them bother you. They will come and go; just keep on keeping on.

People used to ask me if I wanted to be an administrator. Hell no was my answer. I loved the kids, and I had my own kingdom in my classroom. If you want more responsibility or involvement, take a union position. You'll be much better off. Administrators have lost most of the joy of teaching, and that's the point, isn't it?

8
RESPECT SUPPORT STAFF

"We must learn to live together as brothers or perish together as fools."
Dr. Martin Luther King, Jr.

My Uncle, Thomas Tomarelli, served in the newly formed air force, or Army Air Corp as it was known then, in World War II. He came home, went to college on the Government Issue (GI) Bill, and became a teacher. I think he made three thousand dollars a year in his first job. He worked as a middle school Art teacher until he retired at the age of sixty-seven. He loved it.

The most critical piece of advice he gave me, when I started teaching, turned out to be absolutely true. It was to respect the secretaries and custodians. Give them a gift at the holidays and always address them respectfully.

This truly was the best advice he gave me, and here's why. You live and die by the goodwill of the support staff. The nicer you are to them, the nicer they will be to you.

There were twelve secretaries in the building, during the last ten years of my career, and I gave them a gift every winter break. It was my personal challenge to find something affordable and nice that I could give twelve people.

One banner year, in August, I found terrycloth bathrobes down the beach at the Customer Service Values (CVS) store for something like four dollars each. It was the end of the season and they were trying to get rid of them. I made the guy go in the back and get me twelve. CVS was happy, I was pleased, and the secretaries were delighted.

A box of cookies for the custodian, a card with some Hershey's kisses to the parking attendant or lunch lady. These things make people light up when they see you and genuinely grease the wheels when you need a favor or have messed something up. Most important, of course, is treating these people with respect. You'd be amazed how many people don't.

In return, you'd be surprised at the level of cooperation I always had. People went out of their way to be helpful to me. Even the most curmudgeonly secretary or custodian greeted whatever I needed with a smile and helpful attitude. It was to the point where if other people in my department needed something, they asked me to ask for it.

Others noticed how nice support staff were to me. I tried to explain that it wasn't difficult to achieve this, but most people couldn't be bothered. The thing is that everyone is busy. But taking time to acknowledge other people's existence and their work makes a difference in their perception of you and their willingness to work with you.

Support staff are just like everyone else, trying every day to do their best. Help them and yourself by being courteous and, if possible, generous. Conversely, if people are ignorant to you, do not take it. No need to get upset; just let them know that you are not a doormat.

Many years ago, we needed some wood panels for an art show. We needed them from the district's Buildings and Grounds Department. The man in charge of this was notoriously difficult. He screamed and yelled and was intimidating. I grew up in a house where people yelled a lot, so I knew it really didn't mean anything. As long as someone is not throwing punches or things at you, you are safe.

Anyway, my colleagues asked me to go because they knew I didn't scare easily. I made an appointment with his secretary, showed up, and was shown in. When I asked for what we needed, he ranted and raved for a few minutes. I looked him in the eye and said, "Are you done?" He was stupefied. I again made clear what we wanted and why and politely thanked him.

We got what we needed. As a matter of fact, from then on, we always got what we needed from that department. Be polite but don't be afraid.

In short, make your life easier by taking care of support staff. If you can't afford a gift, then a card, a smile, and just plain old respect will make an enormous difference in their lives and yours.

9
HAVE NO FEAR

Teaching is a strange profession. Basically, it is essential to civilization, and maybe that's why people resent it so much. They really can't live without it. The public doesn't like paying for it and doesn't like the perceived power people think teachers have.

Yes, teachers have the power to influence students and the ability to hurt or uplift students' feelings. However, relatively speaking, teachers do not have too much power. Nothing like, for example, the crass power of dictators invading neighboring countries. Ours is more subtle and enduring.

We have become the scapegoats for the ills of society that have little to do with what we do. In my opinion, the lack of skilled and unskilled labor jobs, which have mostly gone to foreign countries, is a big part of why this country has so many problems. But I'll save that for another day.

What one should do to have some power is to join a union if it exists. Collective bargaining is the greatest power, and I have addressed this in a later chapter.

This chapter is about learning to live without fear in the workplace. The first way to do this is by making sure you have respect for others, respect for yourself, and to gain or maintain the respect of the people with whom you deal. Always respect others, no matter their station in life, unless they provide ample reason not to respect them. Always respect your students as individual human beings who have feelings and needs. In return, you will gain their respect.

Don't be afraid to ask for help when you need it. During my second or third year of teaching, I approached my colleagues in the Art Department, all seasoned teachers, and told them I had a problem class. I just didn't know what to do with the students. They were ninth graders, young and hard to engage, and I had run out of ideas and resources. This was before the Internet. They immediately jumped to my aid. People often don't know you need help until you ask for it.

Conversely, one of these very colleagues, a seasoned, highly professional teacher, was assigned a class she had never taught before - special-needs students.

In those days, special-needs students were not always included in regular education classes. They could be a discreet class of their own. She was flipping out. We all rushed in with lessons that would work for these students' levels.

So don't be ashamed to ask for help. We all need it from time to time.

As far as respecting yourself, this is very important. Know your worth. You are not "just a school teacher". You are someone who preserves civilization. You help shape hearts, minds, and bodies. Be a good role model and be someone who people respect in your community.

That being said, do not take crap from people. Stand up for yourself. Not belligerently but in a forthright and respectful manner.

My father once said to me about a job, "They can't kill you; they can only fire you." I found that very liberating. I always stood up for myself, and I was never fired.

People will push you as far as you let them. You need to be fearless. Not in a foolhardy way, but appropriately.

You went to college to become a teacher. You have spent countless hours preparing for this. You know what you are doing. Own it.

10

MEET THEM WHERE THEY ARE

This topic is the most crucial pedagogical thing in this book. Love is the most important overall aspect, but as far as teaching technique is concerned, this is it. It also involves love, but in a different way.

When your students enter your classroom, not only will they have a diverse range of socio-economic and ethnic backgrounds, but they will also possess very diverse skill levels. As an Art teacher, I taught all levels: students with special needs, students with Individual Educational Plans (IEPs), average students, and brilliant students.

We did have leveled classes, but they were filled with students with diverse abilities. So when they came in, I learned quickly to assess where each student was skill-wise and took them from that place to wherever they could go.

I gave whole group instruction, took questions, set students to work, and then checked in on everyone that I knew needed it. Even some students I didn't realize needed it.

Students won't always tell you they don't understand or need extra help. They are embarrassed and feel inadequate. So check to see what the student is doing, either visually or by asking, "You got this? Any questions?".

I once had a student from China, a lovely girl, very quiet. I gave her class a weekly homework assignment. I knew English was her second language, and she was in English as a Second Language (ESL) for support. What she turned in wasn't exactly what I was asking for, but it was close enough, so I let it go. This went on for about a month.

Then I gave a slightly different assignment and what she turned in was way off. At that point, I took her aside and asked her if she had any questions about the assignment. I explained that what she had turned in was not quite what I was looking for.

I discovered that this child had way less understanding of English than I was giving her credit for. She was smart but did a lot of head-nodding when I asked for questions. But she didn't know what I was talking about. I realized I had failed her, and I was ashamed. I was busy, granted, but it was no excuse. So from then on, I went over every assignment with her and stopped taking her head nodding as knowing what I was talking about.

I know many teachers have state or government assessments to deal with and are trying to get everyone to the same place in their subjects. I can only recommend that teachers truly do the best they can, no matter what extra it takes.

I once had a terrific Art student with learning disabilities in the reading and language arts. He was worried about the Scholastic Assessment Tests (SATs) because the school he wanted to attend required a certain score. (Can I just inject here how much I really hate standardized testing of any kind. It does not measure what kind of student a child is. It is an agent saboteur as far as I'm concerned.) Anyway, this was before everyone had computers.

I told the student to get a study book and flashcards and, for half an hour or so, we studied for the SAT every day after school. He took it, got the required score, and got into the college of his choice. It wasn't my subject to teach but I knew he was capable of it. Really it is worth going the extra mile when you can.

To get back to the topic, children progress at different times and in different ways. Developmentally, some students will forge ahead while others take time to get there. The issue cannot be forced. Students' brains don't develop equally. The human brain doesn't fully develop until people are in their early thirties. So it's easy to understand why some students take longer than others. As long as the teacher sees progress, that is what is essential. One must advance them from where they are to as far as they can go.

I once had a student, super-nice, an athlete, and a hard worker. When he started in my class, he could hardly draw. It looked impossible that he should ever pass the course, never mind do anything that looked remotely artistic. Except he was diligent. He did all the lessons and homework, and assignments. I spent a lot of time encouraging him and giving him advice. He absorbed it and ran with it. By the time he left my class, he could draw. He might never have been better than a B Grade student, if one had compared his work's quality with others. But his diligence and hard work really paid off.

I will never forget him because he was like the poster boy for "take them from where they are to where they can go". And his own sense of accomplishment was just wonderful to see. A teacher's job is to encourage, coach, correct, and advise. Never give up on students because one never knows what they are capable of.

Of course, it's easier if students are compliant and want to work. But if they're not, a teacher's job is to find a way in. Over the years I dealt with students who were having psychological issues. Students with bad self-esteem, students with Aspergers who were hard to get to and students who just plain didn't want to be there.

The best thing I could do was encourage them. Being negative never got me anywhere with any student.

I'm not saying teachers shouldn't correct bad behavior. Of course they should and have to. If students work hard but do not accomplish as much as their peers, they shouldn't be punished. They should be encouraged. I'm not saying everyone should get an A Grade, although I honestly have no problem with that. Grades are second to standardized testing, in my opinion, as things that impede learning. The world should not view how well students do, based solely on a test, as a measure of their learning or how hard they try.

If we have to keep giving grades, I think that grading effort, as part of the grade model, is not such a bad thing. I know some people don't like it because they feel it's subjective. But for some students, I think it is the only way for them to succeed. And in life, effort is so important.

Because I taught a subject that no one really cared about, I was able to grade effort, and I was grateful for it. It gave a taste of success to students who had worked hard but were not able to succeed in other classes. More often than not, that success and confidence carried over into the other courses. Once you get a taste of "winning," you don't want to go back.

In short, meet students where they are, then encourage and take them as far as they can go. It's all anyone can do, really, and let the journey be a joyful one.

11
MODERN REFERENCES

When teaching, it's vital to make subjects relevant to the students. Current cultural references are the easiest and most effective ways to do this. For instance, I dissected the video Power by Kanye West when teaching about ancient Egyptian Art. It was loaded with Egyptian Art and symbols. That was, of course, quite a few years ago and might not be culturally relevant today.

For many reasons, as a teacher, you need to be aware of what is happening in the world. More than anything, it is so that you can keep your teaching relevant. With online resources being what they are now, it is easier than ever to do this. Younger teachers and those just starting will be aware of many more resources than I am.

It is super important to bring the world into your classroom, even though field trips are getting harder to come by. I always found that students made enormous leaps in knowledge whenever we took them on field trips, and I am sorry it is so much more difficult to do so now. Whenever you can, please do take them on field trips. It is a lot of work and responsibility, but honestly, the impact is enormous.

Think back on what you remember from school. It won't be the hours spent sitting at a desk. Quite often, the things that remain with you, apart from the social interactions, are what you learned or experienced on a field trip.

There might be small grants from the Parent Teacher Organization (PTO) or other local organizations that you can tap into to pay for things like field trips or guest speakers. Also, look into local museums, Historical Societies, Rotary Clubs, and the like for partnerships or sponsorships.

Other ways to bring the world into your class are with guest speakers. Often parents do interesting work or have hobbies that they are happy to share with the students. Apart from family and friends, business people are another great resource too. Don't be afraid to ask. All people can do is say no. They won't cut you out of a will. More often than not, folks are delighted that you think they are interesting enough to contribute to children's education.

Another way to do this is simple room decoration. I always had at least one poster from a movie that was big with the students that year. I also used comic book superheroes, Marvel characters, etc., to decorate, as mentioned in the Room Decor chapter. What is key is to do whatever appeals to you and can connect with your students.

Be sure to acknowledge what is going on in the world at the time. If something big is happening in the country, be sure to acknowledge it. If a big movie or new music artist is trending, make some reference to them. Find a tie in whatever subject (or subjects) you teach. There is always something if you look hard enough.

When my son was little, he hated the books that his class was given to read in school. He loved History and the TV show Liberty's Kids. So I started taking him to historical sites related to the show. We live outside of Philadelphia, so that was easy. All the sites had gift shops, so I bought him books in the gift shops. He was soon reading like a champ because these books interested him.

I also taught him how to use Wikipedia. For HOURS he read up on subjects that interested him. We kept the computer in the kitchen (desktop), so I knew what he was looking at.

What I'm saying is, you've got to relate things to students to keep them interested. It takes a little time and effort on your part, but it is so worth it in the end. Yes, there are things that students have to know, and it's not always what they want to know. But you can make the path so much easier if you keep it as relevant to their interests and world as you can.

Public Broadcasting Service (PBS) is an excellent resource for this. Some of the shows have free educational guides and other resources on their website. There are many others as well, and a little research will unearth them.

12
TUNE OUT NOISE

There is so much going on all the time. Even if you don't leave your house, you are inundated with texts, social media, television, and other media. In addition, there are announcements, rumors, and basically incessant chatter while you are in school. It is important that you learn to tune out all this noise to be able to get on with your work.

Personally, I have found social media the hardest to put aside. I know there are timers you can set on your computer to cut you off if necessary. I haven't reached that point yet. But even when I was teaching, or trying to get work done in the evening, or over lunch, I couldn't resist sneaking a peek. Then it took me an hour to get back on task.

What you have to try to remember is that nothing on social media is as important as the work in front of you. Teaching your students is an amazing opportunity; seize it.

The other noise that can be disheartening to the profession is the political wrangling around teaching. It just shows that if our jobs weren't necessary, they wouldn't bother trying to control us. So while your community, your state, or your country may all be arguing about how teachers should do their job, my best advice is just to do it to the best of your ability.

In my experience, all their talking, posturing, and gavel-banging generally amounts to nothing. There is no point in worrying about an outcome because there is very little you can do about it. In most circumstances, the best thing to do is pay your union dues and donate to the union's Political Action Committee (PAC). Until they get rid of lobbyists (insert eye-roll here), your best voice in the government comes from the paid lobbyists your union hires.

As for the rumor-mongers in your school, you'll soon figure out who they are, run, don't walk away, run. In another chapter in this book, you'll see that I recommend the same response with gossips who are essentially the same. Every once in a while, a rumor ends up being true. But I must tell you that invariably it doesn't. So just ignore rumors until you get it in writing.

I think the word and concept of mindfulness may be a bit overused. It's one of those words like "self-care" that gets on my nerves. But what I'm essentially talking about is mindfulness.

Be current in the work you are doing, and don't worry about things over which you have no control. Do not worry about what might happen if... There will always be an "if". It is not worth worrying about and will consume you and destroy your happiness.

Try to just be. The idea of "Radical Acceptance" plays into this as well. It's a concept you can research further if you are interested.

13
UNIONS

"Our labor unions are not narrow, self-seeking groups. They have raised wages, shortened hours, and provided supplemental benefits. Through collective bargaining and grievance procedures, they have brought justice and democracy to the shop floor."
John F. Kennedy

If you are lucky enough to teach someplace that has a union, join it. I don't care whether people say they are good or bad; the most important thing they do, if you are unlucky enough to ever need it, is offering you legal representation.

The National Education Association (NEA), the national umbrella union I belonged to, gave me six million dollars of legal fee coverage. You will never have that much money to spend on a lawyer if you are a teacher.

What unions do is negotiate the best contract for you and your colleagues. This may not always seem to be the best contract in the world. But, trust me, they have done the best they are capable of in whatever is the current teaching climate. Your contract is their contract, and they want the best one they can get.

They also ensure that you are not sexually harassed or harassed in general and that your school follows the contract to the letter. What they don't do is take care of your personal issues with fellow teachers and administrators. If it's not in the contract, it is not in their remit.

My first suggestion is that you read your contract, then you will know what the union is capable of helping you with. Occasionally, if you have a good union, they will mediate a meeting if you have a personal issue with a fellow teacher or administrator. Should it become an issue with you doing your job, they will facilitate fixing the problem.

I did this many times as a union representative. It can be informal, so it does not come to the administrators' attention because you really don't want that. You'll become known as a person who cannot get along, and that is not a good thing. If you are genuinely being harassed, take it to your union.

They can't really do much about your room unless it is a Health and Safety (H&S) issue. My advice is to always phrase any room complaints as an H&S issue. It is the only way they will listen to you.

Sometimes you will have great union leadership; sometimes, you won't. I highly recommend you get involved by accepting a position in the union, even a minor one, like sending flowers to people who are sick. You will get to know who everyone is, and they will know you.

Your school will also know you are involved, and that will carry respect with it. Unions need younger, newer people. Their membership comprises teachers, and it's important to get involved and not just pay dues. Don't complain if you don't do anything to make things better. It can be time-consuming and tedious, but I always found it worthwhile in the long run. I didn't get paid anything extra for doing what I did, but it was gratifying nonetheless.

Some positions, like officers, are paid extra and often get released from class time as well. If you really want to get involved, start small and get known. Often nobody is running for these positions, and they are filled by whoever shows up. Get involved.

If you don't have a union but think it necessary, look into starting one. Contact national education unions about getting started. In the meantime, protect yourself by getting to know some senior teachers and asking for advice when you need it.

Teaching can be very isolating. It becomes less so as you get to know others in your building and district. Try to think of it as a cooperative rather than an individual pursuit. Having the support of your fellow teachers is very heartening and will make you better at your job.

14
BEING ORGANIZED

Teachers are told and taught that they need to be highly organized to succeed. I have a confession to make. I am not the most organized person in the world. One look at my house or my classroom will convince anybody of that. I do generally know where things are, but it's very much idiosyncratic, a sort of organized chaos.

What I am is good at finding systems that work for me. For instance, the high school where I taught had a four-day schedule. Each day had different teaching periods, and the morning and afternoon rotated in different cycles. You skipped a different period each day.

It made it better for not getting bored, and you didn't have the dreaded "oh no, my 8th period is a nightmare" scenarios. But it was very difficult to keep track of. So I printed out my schedule for each day, laid out in blocks. Then I made copies for each room I taught in. (Did I forget to mention I taught in different rooms for different subjects?)

Then I hung the schedule beside each teacher desk in each room. That way, I could always SEE where I was supposed to be and what room and subject I was teaching next.

The other system I invented for myself was never to let an email go unanswered until the next day or leave required paperwork until the next day. If I did, it would get sucked into a vortex and not happen.

I made file folders from folded pieces of paper and wrote the class period on each one. Then I stored that IN THE SAME PLACE EVERY YEAR. Into those folders would go each class's work. I pride myself on never losing a student's artwork. Except in one case, but I did eventually find it much later.

Very important is to stay ahead of grading. If you teach different subjects, make due dates on different days, so you don't get everything at the same time. During any given year, I taught anywhere from three to five different sub-subjects in Art. I would put the due dates in my (online) grade book, so I (and my students) could always see them.

When the work came in, I would, within the day, begin to grade the assignment. I often graded over lunch or after school. When possible, I took the grading home. It was just easier for me. What you REALLY don't want to do is let the grading pile up. It annoys the students, their parents, and, in turn, your administrators.

I taught Art, so I would often have verbal critiques. The students would line up their work in the hall, and we, as a class, would give helpful feedback. This can be applied to many subjects. It helps students know where they are, and you don't have to sit down and grade everything so often.

Before you develop an assignment, think it through. How are you going to grade it? Does it require a grade? How often will you be giving feedback during the assignment?

A lesson plan is more than just getting the students to work. It is also how you have closure to the work. This is especially important with "fun" projects and assignments or group projects. How does one monitor each student's work on a group project? It is crucial to figure this out, so one conscientious student doesn't end up carrying all the weight. Frequent check-ins are usually the best way to take care of these things.

So, if you are an organized person, great! If not, you need to figure out a way to get the required things done. Don't wait on paperwork; it will just build up. It won't go away until you address it. It's important. It's part of your job and will make your life easier and better to remain organized and on top of things.

15
DON'T COMPLAIN

It seems that whenever large groups of people get together for a job, someone always complains. It is the nature of the beast. A little grumbling here and there is normal and healthy. People who constantly complain aren't. They are like a cancer in the building and sap everyone's energy.

I used to work with a woman who, every time I saw her, said, "This place is sick!". Well, soon, I found myself trying to avoid her. Who wants to hear that a place where you spend most of your waking and working hours is sick? Besides, what I was doing and participating in didn't feel sick at all. It felt healthy and positive.

Her constant complaint was as much an attack on what I was doing as on those who were running the show. Because, to me, if you are part of something, it is your responsibility to make it as positive as you possibly can.

Constant complaining brings everyone down. Complainers never change their mindset, and it makes everyone around them either join in or avoid them. It is a morale killer.

Ironically, the people who complain most are usually the ones saying, "Morale around here sucks!" They never realize that maybe they are a big part of the reason.

Constant whining and complaining will ruin your credibility. If that is your default state, then nothing you say will be acted on or taken seriously. It will eventually get you on the radar you don't want to be on.

However, I am not saying play Pollyanna (an excessively cheerful and optimistic person) and make out that everything is great. When something needs to be addressed, it should be addressed. Succinctly and to the person or people who can actually do something about it.

To have your concerns addressed, do it professionally and as briefly as possible. In writing if possible. Administrators are as overworked as you are and would prefer not hearing from you, especially about negative things.

If you have a legit concern, of course, it should be addressed. Just don't go around the building telling everyone about it first. Tell the person who can address it. Either a union rep, an administrator, or a department head. If you get no action, check in with them again. If they seem to be ignoring your concerns, ask why your concerns have not been addressed after checking twice with them. If the answer isn't satisfactory, go over their heads. It is your right. Just make sure your concerns are valid.

Constant complainers are toxic people. Do your best to avoid them. If you can't, try not to absorb their negativity. Just nod, grunt and move on. If you are stuck with them, and can't remove yourself, have a little chat. You might kindly suggest they take their concerns to someone who can help solve whatever their complaints are about. Or even suggest, again kindly, that they might be happier elsewhere. If you explain, gently and patiently, that you can't take their level of aggrievedness on a regular basis, they will usually get the message.

If you are in a toxic building, where complaining is the order of the day, staying by yourself is actually healthier. People will talk smack about you, whatever you do. You really must not worry about it. Remain friendly, but don't engage. Your mental health will thank you for it.

16
ROOM DECOR

This may seem like a frivolous topic and not one that you should concern yourself with much, but that is not the case. As an Art teacher, I always loved decorating my room and making it homey for myself. I spent much of my waking hours in my classroom and wanted it to be comfortable.

For some reason, this became especially important to me after I had my son. I stayed home for two years with him after he was born, and when I returned to the classroom, I just felt I had to make it really like home.

I know some teachers may have restrictions on what they can do in their rooms. I know that some schools are strict about those things, but teachers should do the best they can within their limitations.

I'm going to share a story that will tell you how important this aspect of your professional life is. Then I will provide some suggestions.

About ten years ago, we moved into a brand-new school building. The old one, especially my location within it, was incredibly funky. There was decades of encrusted dirt and dust, no air conditioning, and the pipes leaked and made strange noises.

I was in a building that had been built in 1910, and it housed industrial classes like a wood shop, metal, and electrical shops, an auto shop, etc. The windows went to the ceiling, and I needed a pole to open them. The room was huge, which was terrific for art-making.

While it was really cool looking, it was very industrial. So to warm it up, I had posters everywhere and hung fabric pieces in different spots. I found plants and funky old furniture in thrift shops or around the building. I had an old drinks cart from a thrift shop that I put plants on. Also, a barrister's old bookcase filled with still-life objects, etc.

One of the posters I had up was of Johnny Depp as Jack Sparrow in Pirates of the Caribbean. I had it up for several years. This was before the infamous trial and the allegations of abuse. I always had art posters up but also incorporated popular culture icons too. I had an extremely sensitive and wonderful student who had class with me in this room. I will call her M.

When we moved to the new building, I took many things with me. But we weren't allowed to bring funky furniture, etc. For the first year, our permanent art collection of student work, chosen over a period of thirty to forty years, was not allowed to be put up in the hallways. Everything was stark white, clean as a whistle, and impersonal as a trip to the Department of Motor Vehicles.

In about the second week of class, we were all sitting around talking about being in the new building, how impersonal it was, and how it affected everyone. M looked at me and, with tears in her eyes said, "Nothing is familiar, nothing feels the same; I feel lost and scared. You don't even have Johnny Depp up in your room!"

Well, I hadn't put up Johnny Depp because I thought he was out of fashion and figured, new building, new posters. I said, "Oh my goodness if Johnny Depp will make you feel better, you've got it!" I ran to the drawer, pulled out the poster, and put it up right then and there. She had such a big smile on her face and seemed so relieved. M is now a teacher herself and a more kind and wonderful teacher you will never find. My point is that you never know what will resonate and make a student feel comfortable.

To this end, I always hung up art from different cultures. Lots of Black artists, Latinex, Asian, as well as Western Art. I'd make posters of fun little sayings I'd picked up and quotes from people. I would include posters of popular culture, such as current movies or cartoons. All these help make a student feel safe.

If you can pick up interesting furniture and objects on the cheap (or for free) and can bring them in, then please do so. I used colorful bins that had been my son's for toys when he was little, for supplies. I brought in an old armchair and some lamps from home to soften the fluorescent lighting. This was after the first year in the new building.

Also, soften edges. I placed old table cloths over my desk, draped and hung attractive fabric over the whiteboard in the front of the room to soften the edges of its rectangularness. I picked up some fabric with superheroes on it at a fabric store discount bin and used it as a tablecloth to cover a cabinet.

On top of it, I put a basket with current magazines and comic books for students to grab to just clear their heads or get comfy. I only put out things that I didn't mind being taken. I had remarkably few things taken over thirty years, but you don't want to set yourself up to be heartbroken.

I brought in hanging plants and put them in the windows. I used old cafeteria trays to set out plants on countertops and found some small chairs that I put up on the counter to create an interesting plant area. I used funky old cups for pens, and pretty thrift shop finds like vases and glasses (you can use plastic pieces if you're afraid of breakage) to hold bits and bobs. Anything to add color and softness to the harsh white, sterile atmosphere. I would see students visibly relax when they came into my room.

It's not hard, and it's actually fun. Yes, you have to take the cloths home to launder now and then, but so what? Yes, you have to water the plants, but again, so what? You can even make that a student job if you want. Also, allowing students to hang up their work is a great idea. Whether it's artwork or just a doodle they drew, it humanizes the place.

Avoid stuff they sell at "teacher" stores if you can. That rippled cardboard for a bulletin board background? Shudder. And unless you are actually teaching the alphabet, do not hang the alphabet up. It's horrible. It just is, trust me. Also, try to avoid using only primary colors. It's jarring and impersonal.

Cover your bulletin boards with light pastels or even white, then just cover them with lots of great pictures. I also hung up broken pieces of jewelry. Most thrift stores have a box of broken jewelry and will just give it to you. You can put pieces on a string and hang them in the window or on the bulletin board edges, so they catch the light. They will add a pretty, interesting edge to things.

Try to use art and posters that are personal to you. Not bundles you buy from education stores or online stores. I know that for certain subjects you want certain things. So if you do buy a poster set, back them with different color construction paper or something to make them look better.

The personal warmth of your room will help all your interactions with students.

17
P'S AND Q'S

I'm old enough to recall my mother telling me to mind my P's and Q's. I looked up the origin of this expression and found several, so not much help. What it meant to me was, be careful, don't overreact to things, keep your temper. That is what we'll talk about here. Keeping your temper and not overreacting.

I will freely admit, especially when I was younger, that I had a temper. I still do, but I have learned to modify it somewhat. Teaching, while emotionally rewarding, can also be emotionally draining. Add the rest of your life to that, and sometimes it can take its toll. For several reasons, teaching can be frustrating and infuriating too.

Curse word warning in the following paragraphs.

Here's what I want to say. Think before you react. I was not always great at this. Especially faced with a teenager yelling at me several times in a row to go fuck myself. Or by students who wouldn't engage no matter what I did. Or administrators who were being assholes.

But if you react without thinking and say something you wish you hadn't - even as it's leaving your mouth, you're thinking, "Oh God!" - it takes away your power. It really does. Because then you are on the defensive. I'm not saying you can't ever show anger or frustration or never yell at anybody. I mean, just be careful.

I will say that, thankfully, my first and last principal backed me up when these few incidents occurred. They knew my anger was justified even if my reaction was not. I had a few principals in between who weren't so great at that. Fortunately, my son was little then, and my patience was long, so I had no incidents.

I had a real hard time not responding in kind when someone told me to go fuck myself. That only happened twice in thirty years. It was during my first year of teaching and about 5 years before I retired.

Don't put yourself in that position is my point. If I could have just bitten my lip and not responded, the perpetrators would have been punished. Instead, I had to cover my ass and explain what happened. They did not. They, not I, held the power. Not a situation you want to be in.

I found the best way to handle anger was to wait a few beats, mentally count to three, and THINK about what I would say before I said it. Call it "wait time" and add it to your repertoire of tools, especially with students.

If possible, don't cause a confrontation in the classroom. If you can get a student out into the hall, or a corner of the classroom, then do that. Most times, just getting the student out of whatever situation was causing the problem can help.

I would usually start by just mildly saying, "What's going on?" I can't count the number of times students would then dissolve into tears and reveal what was really bothering them. Something at home or some kind of trigger occurring, and it would come pouring out. I would listen sympathetically, then discuss whatever the real issue was with the student. Then I would suggest better ways of acting it out instead of disrupting the class. Sometimes I would send them to their counselor if the problem required it.

Honestly, nine times out of ten, a hallway consultation before, during, or after class was all that was required to solve the problem. I will tell you though, that if you start the conversation in class, you will get nowhere because they have to save face in front of their peers. So always get them away if possible.

I had a student in my last year of teaching, a very attractive girl, a good athlete, polite, fun, and a pretty good worker. Unfortunately, she could not keep her mouth from running during class. I spoke to her in class; just a quick correction like calling her name. I gave her the stink eye. I had hallway consultations. Nothing worked. She was really great at distracting other students from their work, and I could see that while they enjoyed her attention, they also wanted to get on with their work.

I started to wonder if she didn't have some type of mental disorder. Finally, I went to her grade level principal and asked him to call her in when I could be there. I didn't want to write her up; I just wanted her to know it was serious. She was disrupting class, and nothing seemed to penetrate her mind that this was so.

Also, she was a student of color, and I didn't want her to think it had anything to do with her ethnicity. Luckily her principal was a man of color, too, so I didn't have to worry that she would feel ganged up on. He was a wonderful man who was great with students, which helped. He readily agreed to help me.

He knew I didn't want her to "get into trouble," but the situation was untenable as it was. So we met. The principal had already put her at ease by assuring her she wasn't in trouble. We discussed the situation and future expectations. I told her how what she did made me feel and what I felt it did to the class. It worked out very well, and we ended up being very close.

This was a Sophomore class, and they are still so young. I think she thought because my class was open, she could move around, and talking wasn't forbidden. Remember, I taught Art, and it was considered okay to just have a free for all. For some reason, the student didn't accept that I was serious about what I said to her until I took it to the next level. It was all done without rancor, very calmly, and it had a satisfactory outcome.

Students can often feel that you don't like them when you correct their behavior. Of course, we are human, and of course, we like some students more than others. But we should always do our best to never make students think we don't like them. If I corrected students, I would always make sure to have a bit of conversation with them after or share a kind word.

If there was an incident of some kind, restorative practice goes a long way to resolution. Teachers unaware of what this is will find much literature on the subject, online and in libraries, about what restorative practice is and how to make it work for you.

Summing up, remain calm, take a breath and remove yourself for a minute, if you can, from a difficult situation.

All these will be really helpful in minding your p's and q's. It will make your life easier in the long run, and that's what it is all about.

18
POWER

"With great power comes great responsibility"
Uncle Ben - Spiderman

Having power is not something I ever thought about as a teacher, and I'm sure if you asked most teachers, they would say they were absolutely powerless. Except it's not at all true. Teachers have enormous power. Usually, we are just told the opposite, so we never realize it.

Throughout my career, parents told me things like, "Thank you for saving my son; we didn't know what to do with him." And, "You've been such an influence on my child, thank you so much." But you know, I never really believed it. It was nice to hear and all, but it didn't give me any sense of power.

It wasn't until a few years before I retired that I really understood. A student had done something outside of school because I had suggested she should. I was blown away. I remember saying, "You did that because I said so?" She was like, yeah, and looked at me weirdly because I was so shocked. I never felt like I had that much impact, especially outside the classroom.

I must have been an awful teenager because I don't remember doing anything recommended by teachers. I liked some of my teachers, but, to me, they were like Charlie Brown's teacher, just words and sound. I guess that's why I never realized there were students who took my words to heart. I never really paid much attention to my teachers emotionally. This is not the case for many students.

I have a friend and former colleague who wrote a memoir. In it, she recounts several incidents in school, from elementary through high school and college, where teachers said terrible things to her. She speaks of the impact that had had on her. It also made me realize how vital these things are to our students. Everything teachers say and do, whether intended or not, has an impact.

Now we see with all this CRT (Critical Race Theory) nonsense that parents apparently believe we have a lot of power. It's so ridiculous because no one but upper-level social studies in college had ever heard of CRT before. But this is the power that parents imagine we have.

I always wished parents could come into the classroom for a day and see what actually went on. It's like parents have never been to school themselves. We teach basically what we are told to teach. I probably had more autonomy than most, but I also had specific targets I was expected to hit. Our power is there, but it's sporadic and certainly not all-inclusive. It's more about how teachers make students FEEL rather than what they say or what they are teaching.

Just this morning, I had a former student make a comment to me on Facebook. This is part of what she said: "Wanna pop in and thank you again for being so supportive in high school. It really meant the world!".

This student came from challenging circumstances and is now a thriving member of society. I honestly didn't do anything extraordinary; I just felt like I was doing my job. I let her hang out in my room a lot, but I would do that for any student. I listened to her worries and complaints and encouraged her when she was down. Honestly, I would do that for anyone, especially my students.

But to her, at that time, it was important and made a difference. THAT is essentially what I'm trying to say. You have enormous power over how your students navigate the world. Be aware of it and use it wisely. I won't quote Spiderman here. Well, maybe I already have.

19
READING FOR EMPATHY

You may be wondering why a book about teaching would be telling you to read more. The answer is empathy. The more you read, the more empathy you acquire for your fellow human beings.

It doesn't matter what you read. It can be fiction, any kind, or non-fiction, of any type. Just taking the time to hear the author's voice in your head puts you in another's shoes.

In my last year of teaching, I joined an anti-racism group. It comprised about fifteen of us who decided to read books by authors of color to help us expand our perceptions of the world. We mainly were White teachers, but that grew as we got going.

We started with books like I Want to do More Than Survive by Bettina L. Love, Stamped by Ibram X. Kendi, and White Fragility by Robin DiAngelo. They were not easy reads. So often, they said things we did not want to hear.

Except it turned into so much more than that. As the year went on, we stopped talking about books and started talking about, and to, each other. We connected in ways we never would have had we not started reading these books. It was what they said, yes, but also the issues they raised.

That's what books do; they connect you to not just whatever the author is talking about, but they connect you to your humanity; your trauma, your joys, your sorrows, your accomplishments. They ring a chord inside us that lets us see how these emotions and sensations connect us to others. It is said that you are never alone as long as you have a good book. This is true for so many reasons.

The reason this is important is that you need to have empathy to be a good teacher. You need to understand how you are making students feel. This can only happen if you can at least try to understand what they are going through on any given day.

One of my favorite authors, Louise Penny, has a group of sayings she works into almost every book. To me, they are the core of what I'm saying here. "The four sayings that lead to wisdom: I was wrong, I'm sorry, I don't know, I need help." - Louise Penny, The Madness of Crowds.

If you were to ask readers what Louise Penny's books were about, they would probably say, "They are murder mysteries." But they are so much more. They are character studies into why people do things. They are also ALWAYS about empathy. That's what reading does for us. It tunes up our empathy and allows us to see the world from another's perspective, if only for a little while.

Put yourself, for a minute, into the mind of a scared five-year-old or embittered thirteen-year-old while you're dealing with them. It'll change whatever you are about to do.

Think about why they did whatever they did or why they are reacting the way they are.

Empathy is so essential to being a successful teacher. One must be humble yet have confidence. It's not always easy, but reading can definitely help us get there.

20
NOT A CONTEST

My son's fifth-grade teacher once referred to a confrontation she'd had in class and then announced, "I won." I thought to myself, what did you win? Are you in competition with fifth graders? You're supposed to be teaching them, not competing with them!

Instead, I smiled and nodded. It was funny how much my son's teachers revealed to me because I was a teacher too. They said things I'm sure they would not have confided to a "regular" parent. Often, as in this case, it really wasn't what I wanted to hear. But I digress.

The whole point of this anecdote is that you are not competing with the students. They may think it's a power struggle, but it isn't. As unsupported as you may feel, by administration, etc., the classroom is YOUR world. You set the tone and the rules. The system is on your side to "win". So just go in with confidence.

Another important thing you should remember is not to prejudge students or pay too much heed to what other teachers say about them.

Early in my career, I heard about a student entering ninth grade, the grade I was teaching. He was the terror of his eighth grade class, just awful, out of control, a monster, and able to wreck a whole class. Oh Lord, I actually prayed the night before the first day of school when I knew I had this lad coming into my class.

Do you know who showed up? This "terror" was a little boy that reminded me of a chicken. He was skinny and had red curly hair and a beaky nose. He was a goofball, for sure, and could be disruptive. But he certainly was NOT the monster I had been prepared for. I think that because I usually laughed at his antics and honestly felt sorry for him most of the time disarmed him from any ill-intentions he might have harbored.

Another "monster" I was told about early in my career really was a very difficult child. He was large, disruptive, and a little scary. When he couldn't sit still, I had him clean out supply closets for me. This boy WAS very difficult, but he WAS still a child.

I did my best with him. I never sent him to the office, but occasionally I made him sit in the hall outside my door. We had lots of talks. At the end of the semester, when our class was over, he thanked me for being "so nice to him."

Dear God, I almost sat down and cried. I hadn't been nice to this child. How I wished I really had been. I guess compared to how everyone else treated him, I had been nice to him.

Think about that for a minute. Really sit with it. Uh-huh. That's what this child's life was like.

Another story about another "monster". All I heard about was how truly terrible he was. Then this little man showed up in my class. He had cigarette burns up and down both arms from his mom. HIS MOM! I went home from work that first day I met him, and my husband made me a martini. I drank it and I sobbed.

This so-called monster was an abused child, as are so many of the children you will teach. Most don't have external signs to show you. Children are abused even in an affluent school like the one I taught in. Whether by actual abuse, verbal and physical, or most often by neglect. The wealthiest kids are so often neglected because their parents are too busy making money. They don't have time for their children. This was another child for whom a little kindness, compassion, and patience went a long way.

Difficult children come in all shapes and sizes. How they react to you and how you run your classroom can be totally different from how they respond to other teachers.

So no, don't listen to what other teachers say about a student. Form your own opinion, and please do remember that you are not in a competition. You are there to serve and to care.

21 THE ONLY CONSTANT IS CHANGE

> "Heraclitus, I believe, says that all things pass and nothing stays, and comparing existing things to the flow of a river, he says you could not step twice into the same river."
> Plato

So you've finished your education and student teaching and feel ready, willing, and able to take on your first classroom. That's great!

Let me tell you a little secret. Having your own classroom is basically nothing like what you just went through. It is a constantly evolving world of organized chaos. No matter how well you plan, expect the unexpected. Experienced teachers will know exactly what I mean by this.

First, every school within every district is different. You will have to learn the culture of your school and adapt accordingly. By this, I mean how teachers interact with each other, adjust to administrative expectations, and understand the socio-economic makeup of their students. The more you can find out before the school year starts, the better.

As far as curriculum is concerned, whether you're handed a script, an outline, or you make your own, learn how to adapt it to the students in front of you. Each class will be different, and you have to start from where they are, not where your curriculum starts. Assign some pre-assessment to gauge the level of your students. Who needs extra help? Who is flying high?

Make the assessment as non-threatening as possible. I always awarded my students an A if they turned the assessments in. There should be no coaching with the pre-assessment. It's designed to discover what they are capable of doing.

As a teacher, take any opportunities for professional growth. It will help you keep up to date on jargon and new, or recycled, teaching techniques. It's essential to keep fresh, for yourself more than anything, and of course, for your students. Your district or school will offer professional training days. They can be good but sometimes not really what you are looking for.

There are tons of great books out there for resources; just ask your administrators. Mine were always reading them. If they know you are interested, they will often give you copies.

You can take courses at local colleges or online. If you search around, seminars, etc., abound. You can often get salary credit for these as well. It certainly will raise you in the eyes of your school or district, as well as make you a better teacher. Even if you get just one nugget from something, it's enough. It can make it all worthwhile.

One nugget I picked up at a district in-service day run by my union was from an older teacher from another district. He would look up a student's birthday and give them a donut in class that day.

I modified that for the modern world. I got a few packs of the birthday cards from the teacher's store and some nice pencils from Amazon. Then I gave students a card and/or a pencil on their birthdays. In most cases, it meant so much more than the few cents each card and pencil cost me, especially in a high school where things aren't celebrated much. It may seem stupid and simple, and it's certainly not in any education books. But it is part of the human connection teachers should try to make with their students.

During my time in teaching, I saw so many mandates, techniques, and strategies come and go. One would think I had taught for a hundred years rather than thirty. But as society evolves, so does education. The way I taught when I started teaching was markedly different from how I taught thirty years later.

I had a colleague, Russ, who always proposed ways to revolutionize teaching. So many of his ideas were really great and student-centered. Many were also challenging to implement in the industrial, early 20th century model of education we still have today. So we would tweak his ideas here and there, try things out, and see what worked and didn't. It was exciting and kept our teaching new and relevant.

It's vital to maintain progressiveness in one's thinking when teaching. Teachers shouldn't become staid and stuck in what they do. And if you are open to change, it will make YOUR life easier.

Because things are going to change whether you like it or not. It's much easier not to fight it. Adapt it to your style and your student's needs, rather than cling to the past.

22
FORTUNE FAVORS THE BRAVE

> "Fortune favors the brave" - sometimes written as bold.
> Terence (c. 190-159 B.C.) Many sources say that the first recorded use of this ancient proverb was in the play Phormio (161 B.C.), written by Publius Terentius Afer, the Roman playwright known as Terence for short.

Fortune favors the brave has always been one of my favorite quotes. I don't even remember the first time I heard it, but it resonated with me. I don't think I'm unusually brave. I'm not sure I would even want to be. I do know I'm not really afraid of anyone.

I think I'm as good as anyone, as intelligent as most anyone, and as hardworking as anyone. Maybe this is a uniquely American thing, I don't know. I watched many co-workers, over the years, act like they weren't courageous. I want to tell you there isn't any reason not to be.

Don't be afraid to take risks while teaching. They should be good, solid ones that benefit students' learning and well-being. Don't be afraid to be who you are and to let people know who that is. Don't be afraid to speak up when you see something that is wrong. Don't be afraid to change careers if that will make you happy.

At the age of thirty, I was hired to be a teacher. I was glad I had first had some life experience in other professions. It helped me to better appreciate being a teacher. I loved teaching. I loved my students and most of my co-workers.

I always felt privileged to have a job I enjoyed going to. The best thing about teaching was that I could make it a place I enjoyed going to, and I could also effect change. Never think you, as a teacher, don't make a difference. You do. And make sure you have fun doing it.

It is my fondest wish that something in this book may help you on your career path and help make you the best teacher you can be.

Whether you are twenty-one, thirty, or fifty, if you are called to the profession, do go for it. Right now, quality educators are needed more than ever before. So if you wish to become a teacher, please do it.

Love and good fortune to you, brave one.

Thank you for reading my book. This was a labor of love.

ACKNOWLEDGMENTS

I want to thank all of the teachers I ever had, the great ones and the terrible ones, I learned something from everyone. Especially Ron Linder, in college, who was my student teaching supervisor and the best example of a great teacher.

To all my colleagues over the years, at Lower Merion High School, professional and support staff, it was a privilege working with you. Your quest for excellence never wavered. Especially my Art Department colleagues, Susan Jewett, Gladys Freedman, Harriet Ackerman, Russ Loue, Dan Hazel, Ben Walsh and Ben DeMeo.

Also, to my Harriton Art colleagues, always supportive. I'd especially like to acknowledge Butch Smith who was such a great supervisor and he and Jackye have become such terrific friends.

And finally, to Sean Hughes, my first reader who was so encouraging about this book. You were a great principal and an even better friend. Taken way too soon. Thanks for everything Sean.

I would also like to thank Victoria and Joe Twead at Ant Press without whom you wouldn't be reading this. And all my friends at We Love Memoirs for unwittingly giving me the courage to write this.

ABOUT THE AUTHOR

Louise Pierce was a high school Art teacher for thirty years. Before teaching, she worked for eight years in a variety of art-related jobs.

Louise has a Bachelor of Fine Arts Degree in Painting and Drawing from Philadelphia College of Art, now the University of the Arts. She also has a Teaching Certificate from Rosemont College and a Master's Teaching Certificate from the State of Pennsylvania, obtained from several colleges over the years.

Louise's favorite hobby is reading, if one can call reading a hobby. It's more of an obsession. She also likes to garden and travel and making art is of course one of her greatest interests. She feels like she has a fiction book in her somewhere but we'll have to wait and see if it works itself out.

She lives outside of Philadelphia, Pennsylvania, USA, with her husband and son, and a cat named Zoro.

Louise is always happy to answer questions or chat at:

piercelouise15@gmail.com

Or on her Facebook page:

facebook.com/louise.pierce.37

Made in the USA
Middletown, DE
11 August 2022